DK Machines at work

DIGGER

DK

LONDON, NEW YORK, MUNICH,
MELBOURNE, and DELHI

Written and edited by Nicola Deschamps
Designed by Susan Calver
Additional design Helen Chapman,
Jacqueline Gooden, and Cheryl Telfer

Publishing Manager Susan Leonard
Managing art editor Clare Shedden
Jacket design Bob Warner
Picture researcher Sarah Stewart-Richardson
Production Janet Levesley
DTP Designer Almudena Díaz
Consultant J. Bowles

First published in Great Britain in 2004
by Dorling Kindersley Limited.
80 Strand, London WC2R ORL

A Penguin Company

2 4 6 8 10 9 7 5 3 1

Paperback edition ISBN-13 978-1-4053-1535-7
ISBN-10 1-4053-1535-0
Hardback edition ISBN-13 978-1-4053-0239-9
ISBN-10 1-4053-0239-5

Colour reproduction by Media Development and Printing Ltd, UK
Printed and bound in China by Toppan Printing Co., Ltd.

Discover more at

www.dk.com

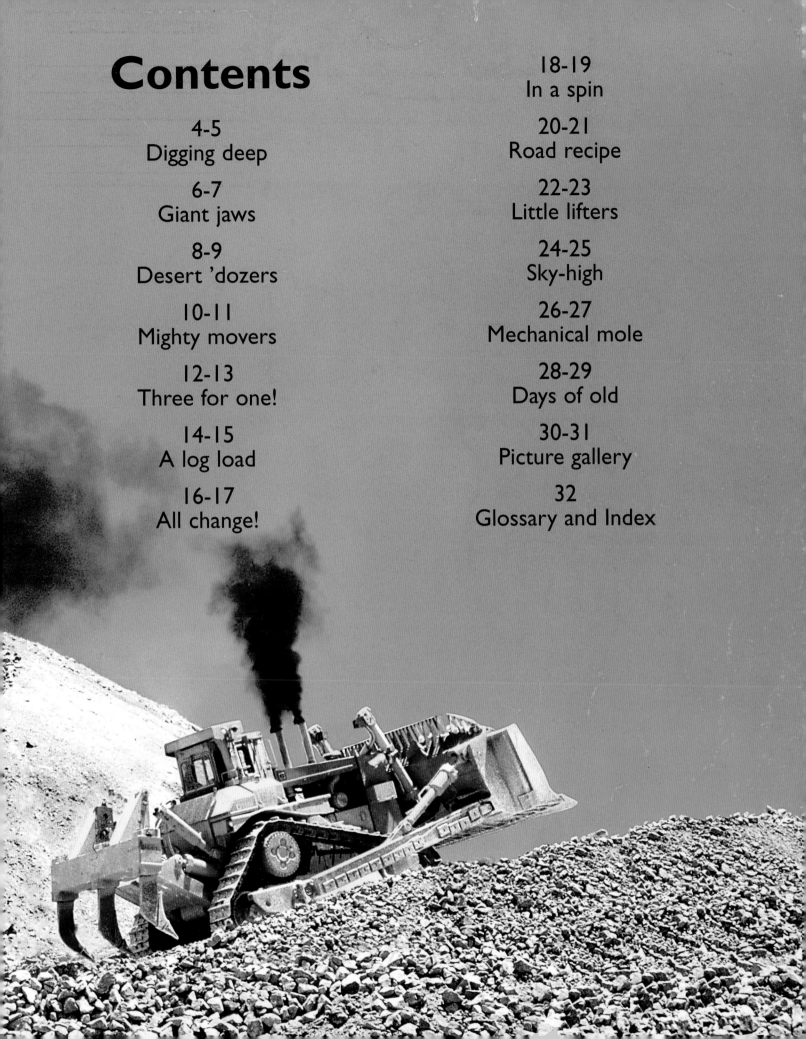

Contents

Digging deep

Excavators come in all shapes and sizes, and there are some that run on **tracks**, while others have **wheels.**

This excavator can run over uneven ground easily and safely on these wide crawler tracks.

Creeping crawlers
A crawler track is made up of lots of separate pieces that fit together to form a flexible band, which is driven by sprockets or wheels.

This big excavator can dig and lift over 13 tonnes (14 tons) of rubble. That's as heavy as three elephants!

Big bucket

This excavator is using a bucket attachment that has sharp teeth. These help it to cut through soil and rubble.

Stick

Boom

Wheelies

This little, wheeled excavator can run almost as fast as a car, so it can be easily transported from one site to another. The boom and stick can be safely folded away while on the road.

It's a fact

The Komatsu PCO1 is a tiny excavator; it's the size of a motorcycle!

A giant mining excavator is so big that the operator has to climb up a stepladder to reach the cab!

Giant jaws

This mighty machine works in the **demolition** industry and can rip apart a house in just two hours! It bites into buildings, demolishing them bit by bit.

This muncher attachment can tear down steel structures and crush concrete floors.

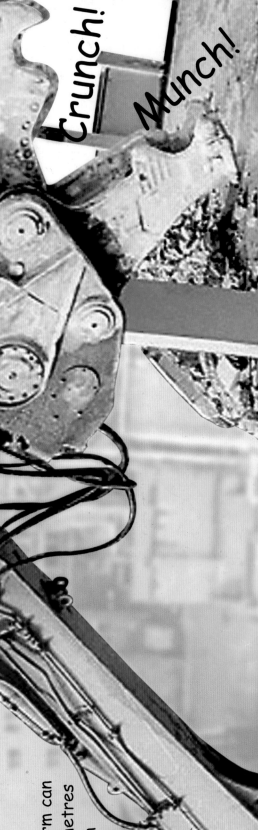

Crunch!

Munch!

Boom!

Explosives are used mostly to demolish high-rise buildings — a 20-storey building can be destroyed in just four seconds!

An articulated arm can reach up to 42 metres (138 feet), which is taller than a 10-storey building.

Old methods

The earliest demolition tool was a wrecking ball, which was used to smash down buildings. It was swung against the side of a building again and again until the building fell down.

Wrecking ball

High-spy

Some long-reach excavators have a camera attached to the top of the arm, which allows the driver to see what the muncher is doing.

A heavy weight, called a counterbalance, stops this machine from tipping over.

Desert 'dozers

Using their huge metal **blades**, bulldozers can **push** and **cut** their way through anything in their paths, even a desert!

These bulldozers are helping to clear sand to make way for canal building.

Up and down
The driver can tilt this bulldozer's blade downwards to cut and push, or upwards to build up a big pile.

Pulling power

With a blade to push aside snow, tracks to grip, and a powerful engine, this bulldozer is ideal for pulling vehicles through the snow.

Rip it up

The sharp prongs at the back of this bulldozer make up the ripper attachment. This is used to tear up the ground ready for levelling or digging.

Mighty movers

Too **big** and heavy to use on roads, this giant dump truck is only found in quarries or **mines** where it carries and **dumps** huge amounts of dirt and rocks.

Hopper
When raised, the top of this hopper is taller than a house, and when the hopper is full, the load weighs more than a jumbo jet!

Load it up
Once an excavator has finished digging it will clear away the rubble by loading it into a dump truck.

Whoooosh!

Liquid motion

Liquid pumped into hydraulic cylinders makes them extend just like telescopes, raising the hopper.

Hydraulic cylinders

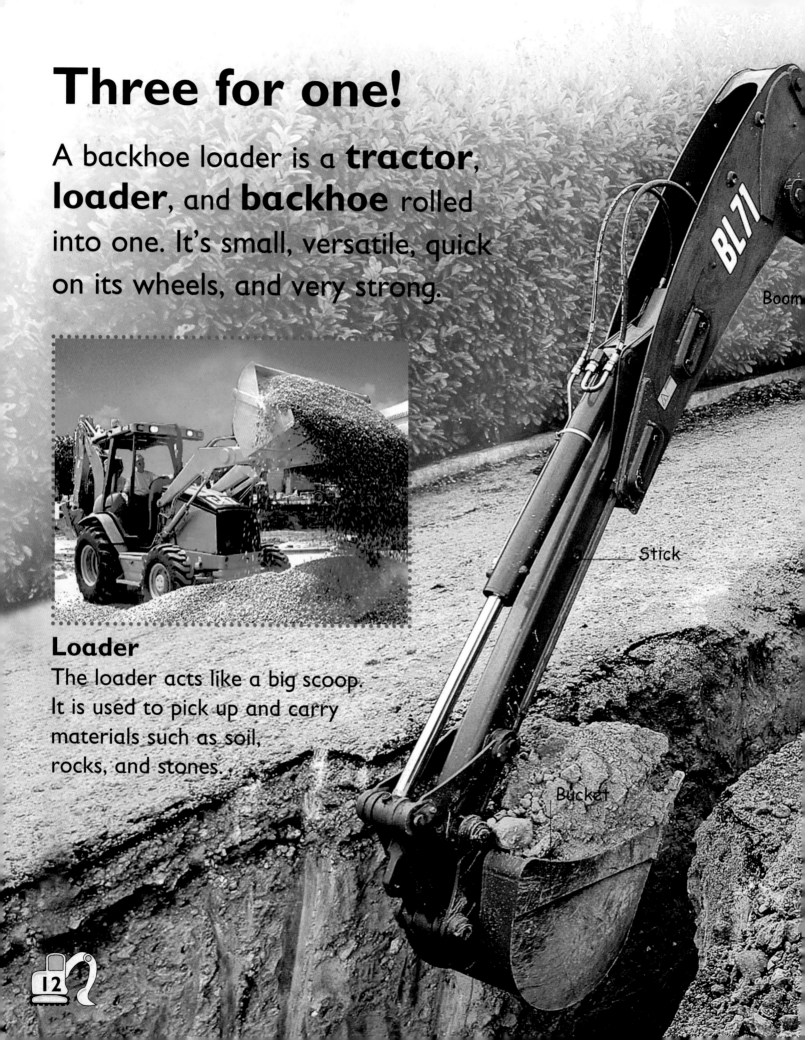

Three for one!

A backhoe loader is a **tractor**, **loader**, and **backhoe** rolled into one. It's small, versatile, quick on its wheels, and very strong.

Boom

Stick

Loader
The loader acts like a big scoop. It is used to pick up and carry materials such as soil, rocks, and stones.

Bucket

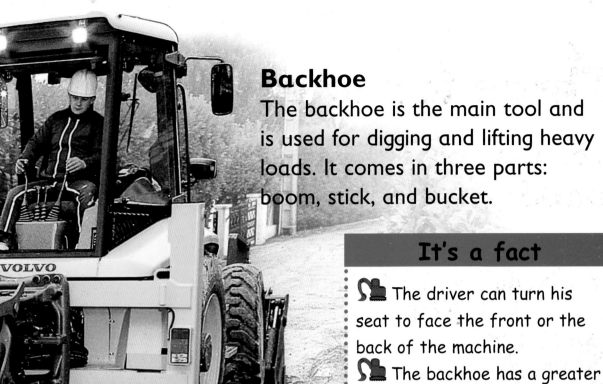

Backhoe

The backhoe is the main tool and is used for digging and lifting heavy loads. It comes in three parts: boom, stick, and bucket.

Stabilizer legs stop this machine from bouncing around or tipping over while digging.

Loader   Tractor   Backhoe

Tractor

Just like a farm tractor, this backhoe loader has a powerful engine, big, tough tyres, and a cab with steering controls.

A log load

This powerful wheel loader is carrying whole **tree trunks** inside its log-grab attachment. It will carry this heavy load to a nearby sawmill.

Scoop, carry, dump

Wheel loaders are used to pick up earth, rocks, and rubble. They then empty their load into the back of a dump truck, which carries it away.

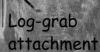

Log-grab attachment

14

Wheel care

A machine's wheels must be kept in good repair. The driver must check that the tyre treads are undamaged and that the air pressure is correct.

Tree treasures

The wood from these logs can be used to make house frames, tables and chairs, or even the paper you write on!

The engine is in the back, which leaves the front free for attachments.

All change!

Can one machine alone dig, carry, crush, drill, and grip? Yes, if it uses different **attachments**, which are easily removed and replaced.

Snap!

Spring clean
With their powerful jaws and sharp teeth, these tough powerclaws can pick up and clear away debris fast.

Steel teeth

Shaker bucket: used to separate a variety of mixed materials.

Grapple: used to grasp and lift objects such as this rusty piece of scrap metal.

Clam shell: used to carry loose material such as stones or vegetables.

Snap!

Break it up

This excavator is fitted
with a breaker. By using this
attachment, the operator
can drill lots of big holes
into a concrete floor.
The more holes drilled, the
quicker the concrete will
crack and break into pieces.

In a spin

The enormous **drum** on this concrete mixer turns constantly to prevent the wet **concrete** inside from setting and becoming unusable.

Chute

Made by hand
Small cement mixers do much the same job as the large industrial concrete mixers. However, it's a builder that loads the raw materials into the drum, and not machines.

Drum

Firm foundations

By using a vibrator, this builder can break up the thick, sticky concrete that has been poured in, allowing it to flow more easily into the gaps.

Mixed delivery

The drum turns one way to mix the concrete, and the other way to empty it out. The wet concrete comes out of the drum and pours down the chute.

It's a fact

Wet concrete is acidic and can burn if it stays in contact with your skin.

The driver can operate the drum by remote-control.

Concrete is a mixture of sand, small stones, cement, and water.

Road recipe

Making a **road** is noisy, dusty, hot, and steamy. Machines must dig, carry, scrape, push, and spread before a road is ready for you to **drive** on!

Blade

Smooth operator
Before a road can be laid, the ground must be made smooth. The top, bumpy layer is scraped off by this grader's metal blade.

It's a sticky business
Lots of steam rises as hot, sticky tar pours out of this paver, forming a new road. Up front, the dump truck keeps the paver supplied with tar and stones.

Dump truck

Chip-spreading

Drum roll
With its heavy water-filled wheels (drums), this roller presses down the new road laid by the paver. Water is sprayed over the road to help it set.

NOTICE
HARD HAT
AREA

Sky-high

Cranes are the tallest machines in the world. They reach high into the sky and can lift massive loads, from huge metal beams to whole boats!

On the move
Fitted to a special truck, this mobile crane can be driven from site to site. Its arm extends like a telescope.

Jib

This is a small gas-production platform.

Floating cranes
Off-shore drilling stations are built with the help of special cranes that are fitted on a huge boat (barge).

Operator's cab

Bird's eye view

From a small cab far above the city skyline, the operator can control the arm movements of this towering crane.

Tower

Crane barge

Mechanical mole

With its huge spinning **head** and razor-sharp **teeth**, this massive tunnel-boring machine can **cut** through earth, under a seabed, or even through a mountain!

Cutting head

It's a fact

This amazing machine cleans up after itself, removing rubble with an internal conveyor belt. All that is left behind is a smooth, clean tunnel, ready for development.

It's a heavyweight
A powerful crane is needed to lift this boring machine into place as it weighs more than 300 cars!

Rocky road
Fitted with 48 tough cutter discs, this huge cutter head can slice through solid rock.

This machine is longer than a football field!

whirr....whirr....whirr....whirr....whirr

Sea trains
Far below the sea, this tunnel-boring machine is busy digging beneath the seabed making tunnels that will be used by trains.

Days of old

Some of the amazing **machines** you see today weren't around years ago – **people** did the work instead!

Many hands make light work

Teamwork was important and everyone had specific jobs to do. It took a lot of people-power to make just one building – look at all these workers!

Hook
block

Steamy days

This old roller is powered by a steam engine. It uses steam, produced by heat and water, to turn the wheels (drums).

Hanging out

To avoid accidents on building sites today, workers must follow strict safety regulations. You would never see a builder taking a ride on a crane today!

Picture gallery

Wheel loader

Some wheel loaders have metal wheel covers that protect the wheels from sharp rocks and stones.

Forklift

Just like the big machines, forklifts must use flashing hazard lights to warn people that they are nearby.

Roller

There are plugs on each roller drum that allow water to be added or removed.

Crane

A computer works out how much a crane can lift at different points along its arm (jib).

Concrete mixer

A mixer's drum must be cleaned out after use to avoid a build-up of hard concrete.

Backhoe loader

The backhoe loader is the most useful machine, on a small building site, as it has tools fitted at the front and back.

Excavator

An excavator can dig on one side and dump on the other because its top half spins all the way round.

Attachments

Some machines have more than 13 different kinds of attachments that they can use.

Dump truck

Giant dump trucks are transported from site to site in pieces as they are too big to travel on roads.

Bulldozer

If a machine gets stuck in the mud a bulldozer can be used to help dig it out or push it clear.

Glossary

Articulated arm has two or more parts connected by joints.

Boom the back part of a machine's arm.

Bucket the scoop of a digging machine.

Counterbalance a static weight that balances a lifted weight.

Chute a channel that directs loose material.

Drum a hollow, barrel-shaped container filled with liquid, such as water.

Demolition the controlled destruction of buildings.

Diesel a fuel used to power engines.

Explosive a material that blows up when lit by an electrical current.

Hydraulic the movement of machine parts that is powered by a liquid, such as oil.

Hopper a container for carrying heavy loads.

Load the material carried by machines.

Engine a machine that burns fuel to make a vehicle work.

Jib the horizontal part of a machine's arm.

Stabilizers the steel legs that stop a stationary vehicle from tipping over.

Stick the first part of a machine's arm just behind the attachment.

Tar a thick, black material used for road-building.

Mining excavator

Index

Picture credits:

The publisher would like to thank the following for their kind permission to reproduce their photographs: a=above; c=centre; b=below; l=left; r=right; t=top;

1 Volvo Construction Equipment Ltd.; **2-3 Corbis:** Lester Lefkowitz; **4-5** Volvo Construction Equipment Ltd., **4bl Corbis:** Charles O'Rear, **5tr** Komatsu; **6-7** Conrad Blakemore: Squibb & Davies Demolition Ltd, **6l Corbis:** Graig Hammell, **7tr Corbis:** Roger Ressmeyer; **8-9 Corbis:** Christine Osborne, **9t Corbis:** Ralph White, **9r Corbis:** Carl & Ann Purcell; **10-11&31bl Corbis:** Paul Steele, **10l Corbis:** Andy Hibbert; Ecoscene; **11tr** Alvey and Towers; **12-13** Volvo Construction Equipment Ltd., **12l** Caterpillar Inc., **13br** JCB; **14-15t Corbis:** Charles Mauzy, **14-15b Corbis:** Lester Lefkowitz, **14l&15tr** Construction Photography.com: Jean-Francois Cardella; **16-17&31tr Corbis:** Raymond Gehman, **16bl** Construction Photography.com: Xavier de Canto, **16bc Corbis:** Colin garratt; Milepost 92, **16br** Case New Holland, **17r** Conrad Blakemore: Squibb & Davies Demolition; **18-19** Construction Photography.com: Chris Henderson, **18l** Zefa Picture Library: M. Idem, **19tr** Construction Photography.com: QA Photos/Jim Byrne; **20-21** Masterfile UK: Gloria H. Chomica, **20l** Caterpillar Inc.: Finning (UK) Ltd, **21tr&30bc** Construction Photography.com: David Stewart-Smith; **22-23&30tr Corbis:** Lester Leftkowitz, **22l** John Deere/ Pharo Communications, **23c Corbis:** Vince Streano; **24-25 Alamy Images:** Peter Bowater, **24tl** Construction Photography.com: Adrian Greeman, **25tl Alamy Images:** Pictures Colour Library.com, **25tr Corbis Sygma:** Eranian Philippe; **26-27** US Department of Energy, **26tl Corbis Sygma:** Polak Matthew, **26cl Corbis Sygma:** Jacques Langevin, **27b** © QA Photos Ltd.: Jim Byrne; **28-29 Corbis:** Bettmann, **28tl Royalty Free Images:** Getty Images, **29tl Alamy Images:** Popperfoto; **30-31 Getty Images:** Per Eriksson, **30bl** Construction Photography.com: David Stewart-Smith; **31tc** Case New Holland; **32-33 Corbis:** Bob Rowan; Progressive Image.

All other images © Dorling Kindersley
For further information see: www.dkimages.com

Acknowledgements

Dorling Kindersley would like to thank Squibb and Davies (Demolition) Ltd, Volvo Construction Equipment Ltd, CNH France, Controlled Demolition Ltd, Komatsu UK, National Maritime Museum, London, Finning (UK) Ltd Caterpillar, and Barloworld Handling Ltd.